Contents

My toys

Every year, there are exciting new toys in toy shop windows. Inside the shop, there are hundreds more!

There are toys for every child – babies, boys and girls.

Can you see a car to push and a doll to cuddle?
What other kinds of toys can you see?
Which toy would you choose?

Toys and Games

Sally Hewitt

W

FRANKLIN WATTS

LONDON • SYDNEY

First published in 2004 by
Franklin Watts
338 Euston Road
London NW1 3BH

Franklin Watts Australia
Hachette Children's Books
Level 17/207 Kent St
Sydney NSW 2000

© Franklin Watts 2004

ISBN-10: 0 7496 5577 1
ISBN-13: 978 0 7496 5577 8

Series editor: Sally Luck; Art director: Jonathan Hair
Design: Rachel Hamdi/Holly Mann; Picture Research: Diana Morris

A CIP catalogue record for this book is available
from the British Library.

Picture credits:
Photography by Ray Moller unless otherwise credited.
The Art Archive: 24t, 27br.
Tony Boxall/MEPL: front cover bl, 8l.
Chapman/Topham: 5.
Michael Doolittle/Image Works/Topham: 19r.
Gill Emberton/MEPL: 10cl, 25l.
Mary Evans Picture Library: front cover bl, 14cr, 19l, 27tl.
Henry Grant/MEPL: 13r.
John Hinde Archive/RPS/HIPS/Topham: 16.
Harald A. Jahn/Viennaslide Photoagency/Corbis: 26.
LEGO, the LEGO logo and the Minifigure is a trademark of the LEGO Group,
here used by special permission: 17t.
Nadia MacKenzie/National Trust Photographic Library: 20.
Monopoly © Hasbro Inc: 10cr.
Jeff Moore/National Pictures/Topham: 9.
Richard Parker/MEPL: 13l, 25r.
Picturepoint/Topham: 18l, 21l, 21r.
Philippe Psaila/SPL: 17b.
UPP/Topham: 3,10tr,11,14cl, 24b.
Chaloner Woods/Hulton Archive: 12.

Every attempt has been made to clear copyright. Should there
be any inadvertent omission, please apply to
the publisher for rectification.

Printed in China

Georgia's favourite toy used to be her teddy bear. Now she likes her in-line skates and her Walkman.

🔍 Be a historian...

What is your favourite toy?
Has it always been your favourite?
Ask your mum and dad what their favourite toys were.

Mum's toys

In the 1970s, when Georgia's mum was a girl, there were all kinds of exciting new toys in the shops.

Frisbee ▷

◁ Space Hopper

△ Etch-A-Sketch

Have you ever seen a Space Hopper or played with a Frisbee?
Do you know how to use an Etch-A-Sketch?

Sindy was a popular type of doll. Georgia's mum had a Sindy. Her clothes were the latest fashion.

The first Sindy, ▷ made in 1963, was called "Weekender Sindy – the doll you love to dress".

🔍 Be a historian...

Do you play with toys that used to belong to your mum or dad?
What toys do you think Georgia's dad played with?
Turn the page to find out...

Dad's toys

Georgia's dad's favourite toys in the 1970s were his skateboard and Action Man. He also liked playing Monopoly with his friends.

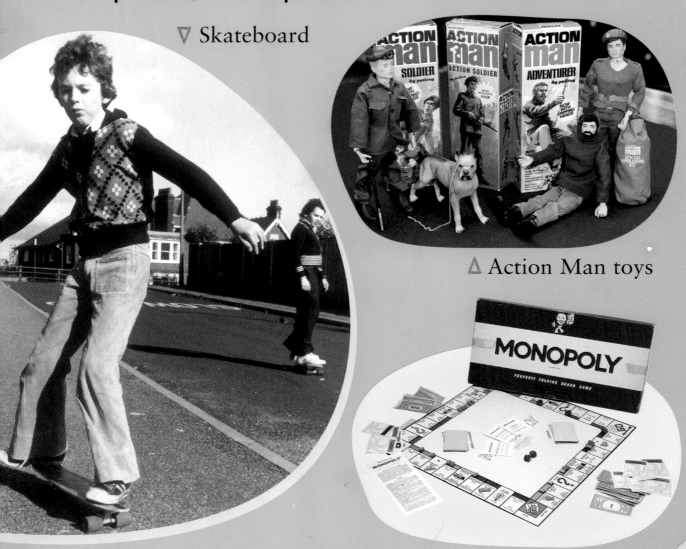

▽ Skateboard

△ Action Man toys

Monopoly (invented in 1934) had been around for many years. Skateboards were brand new!

△ Monopoly

Georgia's dad loved watching television when he was a boy. His favourite programme was Thunderbirds.

He collected Thunderbird toys. Have you got any toys that are from films or television?

△ Thunderbird toys

🔍 Be a historian...

Look at pages 8, 9, 10 and 11.
Which of these toys can you still buy today?
What toys do you think Georgia's granny and grandad played with?
Turn the page to find out...

Granny and Grandad's toys

In the 1950s, when Georgia's granny and grandad were growing up, there were not as many different toys in the shops.

◁ Toys and games from the 1950s

Why do you think children had fewer toys?

Georgia's grandad used kits to make model aeroplanes, and then painted them.
Her granny played board games like Ludo.

△ Model aeroplane

Playing Ludo ▷

Q **Talk about...**

... all the toys you have seen so far.
Use these words to help you:
new   old-fashioned   soft   shiny   colourful   dull

Do you know what toys are made of?
Turn the page to find out...

What are toys made of?

Toys are made of many different materials.

In the past, model soldiers were made of lead. If children put them in their mouths the lead could make them ill.

△ China doll

◁ Lead soldiers

Dolls were often made of china which breaks very easily!

Today, toys are made with safer materials. Baby toys are washable. They do not have small parts which can be swallowed.

The toys shown here are made of wood and plastic. Why do you think they are safe materials?

△ Baby toys today

🔍 Be a historian...

The first plastic toys were made about 60 years ago. Look through the book and find all the plastic toys.

Do you know how toys are made? Turn the page to find out...

Making toys

Toys used to be made by hand. It took a long time to make each toy.

◁ Making toys by hand, 1945

Some toys today are made by hand but they are often expensive. Can you think why?

Q Talk about...

... making toys by hand.

Use these words to help you:

carve	cut	stick	sew
nail	paint	stuff	shapes

Today, most toys are made in factories. Thousands of plastic toys can be made quickly and cheaply from one mould.

△ 1. Tiny plastic chunks called granules are fed into pipes.

△ 2. The granules travel along the pipes to machines, where they are melted.

△ 3. The melted plastic is moulded into Lego bricks.

Can you see how the Lego bricks are being made?

On wheels

Children have always loved whizzing along on toys with wheels. The first pedal cars for children were made to look like real cars.

▲ Pedal car from 1947

Pedal cars ▷
today

Modern pedal cars are made of bright plastic. You won't see cars on the road that look like these!

In the past, children rode along the pavement on big, wooden scooters. Today, children have scooters they can fold up and carry around in a bag.

△ Scooter 100 years ago

△ Scooter today

🔍 Be a historian...

Look at the old and the new scooters.
What is the same about them?
What is different?
What other toys have wheels?

Indoors and outdoors

100 years ago, children who lived in big houses had playrooms. They had to wash their hands before they played with their toys.

A playroom as it would have looked 100 years ago ▷

Q Talk about...

...what you think it was like to play in this playroom.

Use these words to help you:

clean   tidy   careful   fun   exciting

Children who didn't have playrooms played outside in the parks and streets.

Playing with conkers ▷

Games like conkers and skipping were very popular.

◁ Skipping in the street

🔍 Be a historian...

Is it safe to play on the street today?

Was it safer to play on the street 100 years ago?

Do you play games like the ones on this page?

Teddy bears

Teddy bears are named after Teddy Roosevelt. He was President of the United States of America 100 years ago. He saved a brown bear cub from hunters.

Why do you think children love teddy bears?

◁ Early teddy bear

Talk about...

... teddy bears. Use these words to help you:

soft	cuddly	friendly
furry	stuffing	favourite

The first teddy bears were made with mohair (goats' wool) and stuffed with wood shavings. Modern teddy bears can be put in the washing machine.

◁ 1970s teddy bear

▽ Modern teddy bear

Be a historian...

Which of the teddy bears here could belong to your grandparents?
Which could belong to your parents?
Which could belong to you?

How can you tell who toys belong to?
Turn the page to find out...

Toy detective

You can be a toy detective and work out who these toys might have belonged to. You just have to look for the clues and ask the right questions!

▽ Clockwork toy car

△ Scalectrix

One of the two toys belonged to a boy in the 1950s. Not many toys used electricity to work back then.

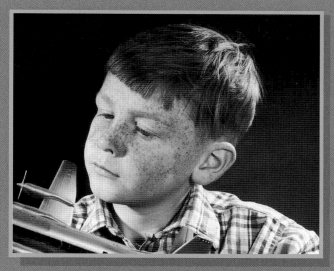

△ A boy from the 1950s

△ A boy from the 1970s

One of these toys belonged to a boy in the 1970s. By then, lots of toys had been invented that used electricity.

🔍 Be a historian...

Read the clues above, then ask these questions about the toys on page 24.
What makes them move?
What are they made of?
Do they look old or new?
Which of the two boys might they belong to?

Make a toy museum

In a toy museum, toys are sorted into different groups. You may find groups of cars and trucks, board games or dolls.

△ A group of dolls in a toy museum

⌕ Be a historian...

Visit a toy museum near you.

How old is the oldest toy?

Which toy would you like to own?

Toys can be sorted in different ways. Can you point to these toys in order of age, starting with the oldest? How else can you sort them?

Make a toy museum with your friends. Collect all kinds of different toys and put them on display.

Timeline

1900s
Toys are made of natural materials such as wood, metal and cloth.

1903
The first teddy bear is named after US President, Teddy Roosevelt.

Start

1934
The board game Monopoly is invented.

1960s
Sindy dolls and Action Men arrive in the shops.

1950s
Plastic becomes a popular material for toys.

1979
The first Sony Walkman is invented.

1976
The skateboard craze starts.

1980s
Video and computer games are used in the home.

1990s
In-line skates and folding scooters become very popular.

2000s
There are more toys in the shops than ever before. What toys do you play with?

End

28

Glossary

Battery
A small pack that stores electricity. Batteries power toys that move.

Board game
A game where two or more players move pieces around a board to win. Ludo and Monopoly are board games.

Electricity
A kind of power that comes into our homes through wires or is stored in batteries. Some toys are plugged into electric sockets.

Kit
A modelling kit has pieces which you put together to make a model.

Materials
What things are made of. Wood, plastic and metal are all kinds of material.

Plastic
A kind of material made in a factory. It is tough and light and easy to keep clean.

Popular
If something is popular, lots of people like it.

Index